The Boy Child is Dying:

A South African Experience

Judy Boppell Peace

InterVarsity Press
Downers Grove
Illinois 60515

© 1978 by Inter-Varsity Christian Fellowship
of the United States of America

InterVarsity Press is the book-publishing division
of Inter-Varsity Christian Fellowship, a
student movement active on campus at hundreds
of universities, colleges and schools of
nursing. For information about local and regional
activities, write IVCF, 233 Langdon St.,
Madison, WI 53703.

Distributed in Canada through InterVarsity
Press, 1875 Leslie Street, Unit 10, Don Mills,
Ontario M3B 2M5, Canada.

ISBN 0-87784-635-9
Library of Congress Catalog
Card Number: 78-4445

Printed in the United States of America

For Abiel and Jeminah
  who suffer because they are black

For John and Jenny
  who suffer because they are white
  and see

Foreword

These stories of South Africa evoke diverse emotions, of anger, frustration, shame, love. One feels anger that such things should happen to human beings, not because they are dishonest or wicked, but because they are black. One feels frustration because the pace of change is so slow, not only the change of law and custom, but the change of heart—and that means the white heart of course. One feels shame—if one is white—that these things are done in one's name, by one's white Parliament (because our Parliament is all white), that one is a member of the ruling class, whether one wants it or not.

Why should the emotion of love be aroused, but with tears, not joy? In one of the stories Judy Peace tells of the release of twenty-two persons who were "banned," that is, silenced and forbidden to take any part in public life, even forbidden to attend any gathering, even of friends. Most of them had been pacifists before they were banned; now many of them had come to believe that change would come about only by violence.

Judy Peace reflected on the trial of the twenty-two as she sat waiting in the car, and when her black friend Mrs. Ntonsheni rejoined her, she said, "You have been crying." "Yes," Judy answered. "I have been feeling the pain of loving this land."

That pain is felt by many of us. This great and beautiful land of plain and mountain and sky, of desert and grassland, of wild flowers innumerable that at times can carpet the plain as far as the eye can see, is a land of pain also. Many visitors from many countries come to see me, and many of them say, "Ah, but your country is beautiful," and in their eyes is that look of love and pain that says as plainly as any words, "But why does it have to be what it is?" And that means of course, why do people treat people as they do? And that means, why do white people treat black people as they do? Why do they treat them as things? Why . . . and why . . . and why?

The Boy Child Is Dying tells stories of love and pain, but they are not exaggerated or propagandist. They are painful because they are true, and they will give to people living in other countries a better understanding of our condition in South Africa. That is after all what the writer has tried to do, and in my view she has been eminently successful. Her style is simple and unadorned. Her stories have the ring of truth.

Alan Paton
Hillcrest, Natal, South Africa
April 1978

Preface

My husband, my children and I lived and worked in South Africa for eight years. We grew to know and love many people of black and white descent. We became aware of the tragedy for both the oppressed and the oppressor living in a virtual police state—both sides imprisoned by fear and ignorance.

The stories I have written here are all true. They all happened to me. But you can live in South Africa all your life and not really see what is happening around you. You can have eyes to see and yet not see. I have white South African friends, for example, who will read this and say these things are impossible or, "This is just our way of life, different from yours." I have other white South African friends who know these stories in many shapes and forms. They share the suffering of their land.

When we were leaving South Africa to return to the United States, a black friend said to me, "Judy, if you can help people in America to understand a little of the suffering we experience every day of our lives as black South Africans, your time here will have been worthwhile."

My hope in writing these sketches is that a few more people will have a compassionate understanding of that suffering and that this will lead to redemptive action. They are not meant to point a finger at South Africa as the most terrible of nations. A black American assured me he could write similar stories of his life in the United States. And I have friends who have been discriminated against in African countries because they were white. These stories are about South Africa simply because that is where these events took place.

Most of the names have been changed to protect people's privacy. The conversations are as I remember them. Not having an infallible memory, I trust they remain true to the spirit, if not the letter, of the words that were spoken.

1

She stopped speaking, looked at me and said, "Yes, I'll work for you."

Startled, I realized who had been interviewing whom. She had been introduced to me as Esther. "What is your last name?" I asked.

"Why do you want to know?" she responded.

"Simply because I am twenty-five years old, you are at least fifty and I would feel very uncomfortable having you call me Mrs. Peace while I called you Esther."

"I am Mrs. Esther Ntonsheni." She

paused. "Mrs. Peace, I worked for a woman
for ten years and she never knew I had
any other name than Esther."

We had been in the apartment for a month.
Having someone help me with my housework
was not easy. I had always done my own
work. I felt guilty watching someone else
do it. Dick and I had decided that, for us, not
having help was irresponsible. South Africa
has something called "job reservation."
Though this is breaking down slowly, for the
majority of the black population it means
finding a job is very difficult. And working
as a house servant is still one of the easiest
jobs to find. Since so many people need
work, we reasoned, the least we could do
was hire someone to help us.

We knew the "normal" working conditions.
We had been told twelve rand (around
seventeen dollars) a month was a good
starting salary. Most people expected their
servants to arrive around 7:30 A.M. and leave
by 6:00 P.M., if they didn't live in. Servants
considered themselves lucky to get an afternoon off a week. Many people felt they
were being generous to give this, as it meant
"managing on their own" that afternoon.
We decided to ask Mrs. Ntonsheni to work

a five-day week, from nine to five, with
a salary above the norm. Perhaps this
was one way of showing people around us
new working possibilities.

Mrs. Ntonsheni entered the room. "Mrs.
Peace, are you unhappy with my work?"

"No. Why do you ask?"

"Well, you are always doing it for me.
I would prefer it if you left it to me!"

"I had not been sure how much to expect
you to do, and I didn't want to overwork
you," I replied, feeling slightly defensive.

"You are paying me a fair wage, giving
me good hours and I want to feel I am earning
my salary!"

Mrs. Ntonsheni took over the housework.

It wasn't more than three weeks later
that Mrs. Ntonsheni said, "Mrs. Peace." I
had come to recognize the tone. She had
something to say. It was going to be difficult
for her. She sounded defensive. "What have
I done now?" I thought.

"Mrs. Peace, I have worked for white
women many years—more than twenty. I was
taught as a girl how to be in a white house.
All the madams, they tell me I am a good
servant. I do all I was taught for you. I think

you don't like it. Why?"

I took a deep breath. I am not known
for hiding my feelings and I too had been
frustrated by our relationship. She was right.
She had played the role of perfect servant,
always "happy," constantly ready to please
us. We could not have asked for more
from a servant, and I assured her of
this. "You do your job wonderfully well,
Mrs. Ntonsheni. I couldn't ask for a
better servant. Every morning, you are here
punctually. 'I am fine,' you answer in response
to my greeting. Your life is always fine. Yet
I see traces of worry in your eyes. I see
signs of suffering. I know your life cannot
always be fine. You work hard, too hard.
It is impossible to get you to rest. You feel
guilty just sitting and relaxing for a few
minutes. When I enter the room, you seem
tense and I feel it is kinder to keep out of
your way. Mrs. Ntonsheni, I didn't hire you
to be a servant under me. I hired another
human being to help me with my work. I
don't feel comfortable in the master/servant
role. I'd like us to work at relating as two
women—equals. I'm beginning to understand
a little how hard that will be for you, but
I'd like to try."

A few days later Mrs. Ntonsheni shouted

from the kitchen, "Mrs. Peace, are you busy?"

"Not very. Why?"

"Well, I'm ironing and it is starting to rain and there are clothes on the line." A long pause.

"I'll get them," I said, as I left my letters and went out the back door, grabbing the clothes basket from the kitchen corner on the way.

"Whew, that rain is really coming down." I stamped my feet, shook my hair and plopped down the basket. Mrs. Ntonsheni gave me a long, searching look. It was no light thing she had done. I appreciated the risk she had taken and the beginning of trust it showed.

"Thank you," I said.

She nodded and I left the room.

2

We were guests for a week in the home of kind, generous people. One evening I was making some punch for dinner. Gloria, the servant, was watching.

"It looks good," she said.

"Here, try some," I said.

"She can't have that!" Linda, the daughter of the household, objected.

"I made it and I'd like to give her some."

Silence, a bewildered look, then: "If she must have some, she can't drink out of *our* cups, she will have to go to her room out back and get her own tin cup!"

"That seems rather silly when there are plenty of cups here," I said as I handed Gloria a cup of juice.

No mistaking the look of fear in Gloria's eyes. But as we looked at one another, her face broke into a half smile and she drank the juice. Linda looked unhappy, ashamed, confused, not knowing why Gloria shouldn't drink out of their cups.

3

William was puttering around the garden. He had "a room" at the back of the property, provided by the landlord as part of his pay for keeping up the yard. I suspect his quality of work was in direct proportion to his estimation of his own value as a person, which wasn't very high. He glanced sideways at me as I sauntered up.

"My wife may be coming to stay tomorrow. Her time is near for the baby to come and I want her close to me and to a hospital. Do you mind?"

William was asking much more than if we minded. It is against South African law for a black man and woman to live as man and wife in a "white area." They might begin to believe they belonged there. The police raided servants' quarters periodically to be sure no "illegal natives" were on the premises. If a man's wife was found with him, she could go to jail and the occupants of the "white house" could be fined fifty rand for "harboring people unnecessary to the area."

"William, I'm glad she is coming. We will help watch out for her."

One night, not long afterwards, Dick and I were awakened by a sharp, insistent knock. William stood wringing his hands. Victoria, down on her hands and knees, was wild-eyed, frantic with pain.

"Get her on the bed," said Dick. "I'll

call the ambulance.''

He and William, feeling their part of the job was over, disappeared into the living room.

Victoria was beyond reason. She grabbed me around the neck and seemed quite capable of strangling me.

"Victoria, let go and listen to me," I shouted. I had just had our first child by natural childbirth so the method was familiar to me. "I can show you a way to breathe that will help the pain. You can control yourself and make this a lot easier!"

We both felt desperate enough to try anything and before long she was huffing and puffing regularly.

The baby arrived as the ambulance pulled up. We were greatly relieved, for the baby was born still encased in the sack and neither Victoria nor I was sure of what to do.

"Thank God you're here," I said to the two white men at the door. "The baby has been born, but something is wrong. We need your help."

"If the baby is born, we'll be leaving, lady. Our orders were just to pick up a woman in labor!"

"Do you know how to save that baby?" I asked.

"That's not the question, lady. You see,

legally, we were called to take a black woman in labor to the hospital and—"

"I don't care about legalities. If you don't get in there and help that baby, I'll have it in every paper in South Africa and America that you two are murderers." This I said very quietly, as I blocked the door with my arm.

Once the baby was out of danger, the men agreed to take Victoria and the baby to the hospital where the cord would be cut, as they did not see this as their responsibility. I wrapped the baby up for protection against the night air. The men refused to touch her once they had dealt with the sack. As they carried the stretcher out, one of the men turned to me and said, "You must be new to this country, lady. Your attitudes will change!"

I sat deep in thought for a long time after they left. It was hard for me to believe what had just happened. I think I had always felt it was instinctive to save a baby's life if you could, but these men *had not wanted to*.

Late in the morning I answered a knock at the door to find Victoria standing there with her baby.

"What are you doing here?" I asked.

"The hospital was too crowded. I was lying

on the floor in the hall. I was hungry and no one had fed me, so I walked home," she said. The black hospital was about a half-hour's drive from our house.

As I was fixing lunch, I glanced out the window. Victoria was filling a bucket at the water faucet. I rushed out to the back yard.

"Victoria, you shouldn't be carrying a heavy bucket. Why don't you get William to do it for you?"

"He is busy, and this is woman's work. I need the water to wash myself and the child. The baby needs water to drink too."

I felt a twinge of guilt that it had not occurred to Victoria to ask me for help.

"You should get help. You could hurt yourself carrying heavy loads now."

Victoria shrugged, shifted the bucket and pushed the door open with her shoulder.

"One does what one must."

A year later I again opened the door to discover Victoria standing there. She had come to show us Tandi, a beautiful, bright one year old.

"Victoria, she is so bright," I said.

"Yes, isn't that a shame," she replied. Victoria knew that to grow up bright and black in South Africa is to live a life of perpetual pain and frustration.

4

Benjamin made a face as he put down the cup.

"Judy, I am truly glad I tried Turkish coffee tonight. Now I never have to drink it again in my entire life!"

The laughter rose and fell. We all settled comfortably into our armchairs.

"Benjamin, you must bring Rachel with you next time you come. I'm looking forward to getting to know her."

A flicker of pain crossed his face. "She won't come, Judy."

"Why not?"

"She is afraid."

"Of me?"

"Yes, of you and all you stand for. She has never related to a white woman in any role other than master/servant."

"*You* are not afraid. Why?"

"I grew up in Lesotho and have had white friends. I have chosen to work with white men in South Africa in the hope of helping bring about change. But it is very hard, even for me."

"Benjamin, what can I do? You and Dick work together. You tell people love can conquer all barriers. Yet you say your wife is afraid to enter my house as a guest. This makes a mockery of your own hope. Rachel and I must meet."

Benjamin's furrowed brow indicated concentrated thought. "Judy, you must begin where Rachel is and she is afraid to enter your home as your equal. She wants to improve her English. Perhaps if you could work with her in a teacher/student role, it would give her more security in meeting you. It would be up to you to make it into something more."

Within a week, Rachel arrived for English lessons. We solemnly opened the grammar book and began. Her English was poor and progress slow.

"Rachel, would you like some lunch?" I asked, when we had been studying sentences long enough.

"Please don't bother, Mrs. Peace."

"Rachel, if you call me Mrs. Peace one more time, I shall be forced to begin calling you Mrs. Mthsali. Both of us being around twenty-six years old, that seems silly!"

The words were wrenched out against the will—"All right . . . Judy."

I left her to go and prepare lunch. A few minutes later Mrs. Ntonsheni entered the kitchen. Looking up, I asked what was wrong.

"Rachel is terrified of eating lunch with you, Mrs. Peace. She asked me to get her out of it. I told her not to be afraid, that you won't bite."

Two years later, we were staying in Johannesburg. Dick's work had taken us there for a year. Benjamin and Rachel were having dinner with us. They too were in the city of gold. We were discussing Mrs. Ntonsheni's relatives.

"They all want to see Mrs. Ntonsheni while she is here, so I suggested she have them over for dinner," I said. "Dick and I made arrangements to be out that afternoon, as Mrs. Ntonsheni felt they wouldn't come if they knew we would be home. She said they would be afraid of eating with us."

Rachel looked at me. "I know how they feel," she said.

5

South Africa is lovely beyond description: open veld, rolling hills, grand mountains, rugged coastline, flowers and foliage beautiful to behold. To explore and experience the sheer lushness and infinite variety of the land is pure pleasure. We spent delightful days trekking through game reserves, canoeing down quiet rivers, climbing mountain trails, searching out bushman paintings and hidden springs. The beaches of South Africa are some of the finest in the world, miles of white glistening sand bordering the warm waters of the Indian Ocean and the harsher waters of the Atlantic. Here are places to relax and be refreshed.

"Mrs. Ntonsheni, would you like to go to the beach with us this Saturday?"

Eyes sparkle. "I've never seen the ocean. Yes, I'd like to go."

"You have lived forty miles from the ocean most of your life and have never seen it?"

"Never had a way to get there." Her

eyes slowly dulled. "I can't go with you,"
she said. "For a moment I forgot."

"Why not?"

"I'm not allowed on the white beaches.
You would have to drive ten miles out to the
'non-European beach' and leave me there. I
wouldn't enjoy being alone in a strange place.
I would be allowed to stay with you on the
white beach as nanny to the children, but
people would stare at me. I would feel
uncomfortable. I wouldn't be allowed to
put my feet in the water either. No, it is
impossible for me to come with you."

Saturday came and we went to the sea.
The relaxing warmth of sun on sand felt
uncomfortably hot that day. The simple
pleasure of play on the beach had become
an escape from the harsh realities of a
sick society, a place for the ostrich to stick his
head in the sand.

6

The dinner was good, the company
pleasant. We took our after-dinner coffee to

the garden, loath to miss the last light of the warm summer sun. One of the men was speaking.

"Heard a story the other day that illustrates perfectly the lack of intelligence of our Kaffirs. Seems there were three boys who thought it was time they each owned a suit. One of those boys made a decent wage; the second was working part-time; the third had no job. The first month the two working boys pooled their money and bought a suit for their friend out of work. The second month they bought a suit for the part-time worker. The third month they bought a suit for the full-time worker. Now any man with a slight bit of brain should have figured out that if he were making the most money, he would be far ahead just buying a suit for himself!"

Laughter . . . the gentle laughter of a fond parent amused at the antics of a child.

It was the Christmas season. Sarah, a friend and frequent visitor, had dropped in for tea. Sarah, Mrs. Ntonsheni used to say, did not act as if she had been raised in white South Africa. The two had become friends.

"Mrs. Ntonsheni, what do you want for Christmas this year?" Sarah asked.

"Sugar."

There was a twenty-five pound bag of sugar in the car when I drove Mrs. Ntonsheni home for Christmas weekend. When she returned, we talked about the festivities we had enjoyed with our families.

Mrs. Ntonsheni turned to Sarah. "We all enjoyed the sugar. It made the Christmas meals nicer."

"What do you mean, 'enjoyed,' " I asked. "You couldn't have finished that bag in three days."

"We gave a cup each to the people who live around us. It is gone now."

"That sugar could have lasted you for months, Mrs. Ntonsheni. Now you have none. Why did you give it all away?"

"We couldn't have enjoyed sugar for Christmas if we had hoarded it, knowing our neighbors had none, could we?"

7

She swung through the gate in a hurry. In her preoccupation, she left it open. There was no mistaking the fear. Its single, overriding power had blocked out all other sensations. The fear was focused with fanatical narrow-mindedness on the inert bundle in the girl's arms.

Mrs. Ntonsheni dropped the cup back into the soapy water as she heard the sharp cry from the yard. When she returned to the house, she brought the fear with her. It was catching.

"It's the baby, Mrs. Peace. I told her not to take him to the witch doctor. She says his cough was worse today. She had no money for the hospital and the hospital is slow and she would wait most of the day for help. The witch doctor lets you pay him later when you have some money. The hospital wants the money now, before you see the doctor. But I told her not to take her son to the witch doctor. The witch doctor is sometimes good, sometimes bad. Now my grandson is very bad. He looks very bad. My baby, my beautiful baby boy!" Her voice rose and fell, rose and fell and finally broke into the wail that the words had been holding back.

Dick had left his study to investigate when he too heard the cry from the yard. He entered the kitchen now, pale and worried.

"We must get the child to the hospital at once," he said. "His condition is critical."

In that moment we felt helpless and angry

before the stupidity of apartheid. The white hospital is within five minutes of our door. The black hospital is a half-hour drive. The white hospital will not accept blacks under any circumstances.

The child, the mother, Mrs. Ntonsheni and Dick piled into the car. The sounds of gears forced into reverse, running feet, the creaking of the gate opening wide, rubber against gravel as the car backed up: the journey began.

How long is a half-hour? Long enough to listen for a heartbeat that gets fainter and fainter, long enough to feel the dear hot chubby hand go limper and limper, long enough to wipe over and over again the beads of perspiration from the smooth brown forehead and the thick curly black hair, and more than long enough to look into the once bright eyes—large brown beautiful eyes—that friends were always exclaiming over—eyes that grow dull and disinterested as the car speeds over the concrete. A half-hour can be a very long time.

Dick let out the women and the child at the emergency exit and parked the car. When he entered the hospital, he found them at the end of a long line winding down a corridor.

"Why didn't you go to the front of the line? The baby cannot wait."

"We did," said Mrs. Ntonsheni. "We told the man our child is very sick, we need help now. He said all these people wait for hours. We wait too."

Dick felt the anger again, but not the helplessness. He marched them up to the man guarding the door. Inside was the overworked doctor.

"Look at this child," he said to the man. "You can see his condition. This baby is dying! If he waits at the end of the line, it will be too late! The child is dying, don't you understand?!"

The man set his chair on all four legs, looked from one face to the other, hesitated, shrugged and let them pass. Dick's white skin had won.

As they entered the room, they said to the doctor, "We have a baby, a boy child, who is dying."

The boy child was not dying. The boy child was dead.

8

We pulled into the drive-in restaurant.

We stopped at one as often as possible when Mrs. Ntonsheni was in the car. We could not go into a restaurant together—one of the inconveniences of "petty apartheid." We ordered and settled back to wait, grateful for the chance to break our journey.

"Which order is for the girl?" the man at the car window asked Dick for the second time.

"Which girl do you mean? We have two daughters," said Dick. Jenny and Lisa romped together in the back seat oblivious to the conversation.

"You know what I mean." The man glared at us.

"No," Dick persisted politely, "I don't know what you mean."

The man took a deep breath. His face was flushed. His discomfort was evident. He pointed accusingly at Mrs. Ntonsheni.

"That girl!" There, he'd said it. He relaxed his breath and almost smiled.

"You couldn't possibly mean Mrs. Ntonsheni. She is at least fifty years old."

"You knew I meant her."

"No, I expected you to know the difference between a woman and a girl," said Dick. "My mistake."

"Which is her order," asked the man.

"What possible concern is that to you?"

Dick replied.

"Natives cannot be served on our regular dishes. She has to have a tin plate and cup." The man was quick to catch the horror and disbelief that crossed our faces. "Nothing personal," he hastened to assure us. "We would lose customers if we didn't enforce this policy."

The man stood alone in the car space as the five customers he had just lost drove away.

My anger sputtered over in irrational statements and oaths against apartheid.

"Mrs. Peace, don't let yourself get so upset. You aren't hurting that man or the system or anyone but yourself. That was a minor incident for me. One of many I encounter in the course of a day. If I allowed myself to feel anger every time I was treated that way, I would be a sick woman by now."

"It was so stupid, so wrong, so humiliating," I said.

"Yes, it was."

"How can you sit back and do nothing? Don't you care if you have to live this way?"

"It is my daily prayer to see this country change. Anything that brings a good change, I am for. But useless anger, destructive violence—that hurts me more than the man who calls me girl."

Years later Dick talked with a man in Cape Town. He was a "Cape colored" who had been thrown out of his home. There was a lovely section of the Cape which had been a colored area for three generations. A community of neatly kept, colorful cottages along the coast of the Indian Ocean. The government decided it would make a nice resort for the white community. The area was reclassified a white area. The colored people, many had lived there all their lives, were moved en masse to a new location: a dry, sandy spot where forty m.p.h. winds whip the sand mercilessly into eyes, nose and throat, making the soulless concrete rooms called homes seem almost havens. The new colored area is miles from Cape Town. People ride buses for an hour to get to work.

"How do you stand this," Dick asked his friend.

"The first year, I nearly went insane. I woke from the little sleep I'd get to a sense of fury, frustration, hatred. There came a morning when I didn't want to wake up. My bitterness had eaten away my desire for life. The injustice that had been dealt me and my people was beyond my capacity to endure. 'This,' I said to myself, 'is not smart. The white men are enjoying our homes. My hatred

is not touching them. It only poisons me.
Once I loved life, now I despise it.' I
decided then that I would look at life again
and accept the gifts of each day. I work all
I can for the coming of a just society for
my land, but I cannot afford the luxury of
hating my oppressors. I think I have come to
pity them instead.''

9

South Africa exists to a large degree by
grace of the mine workers. Without the
revenue from the gold mines, the economy
would grind to a halt. Every year thousands
of black men leave their homes to work in
the mines. The homelands are places of
children, women and old men. The young men
give their youth and vitality away in the dark
underground caverns which yield the precious
metal. When we were in South Africa, they
received in return for the strength of their
manhood approximately a dollar a day.

For eleven months of the year, men are
herded together into dormitories "according to

their tribes." The government claims they are "preserving cultural identities" in this way. It is a small coincidence that it also keeps the blacks of South Africa from feeling a strong national identity. History does continue to move forward, and that national identity is growing in spite of the government's concern for "nourishing one's tribal roots."

All manner of social problems arise from the housing situation. Picture hundreds of men sharing bunks in crowded barracks; some bunks made of concrete with no mattresses. No family life, no male-female relationships, no nurture from the earth each lived with most of his childhood. Much crime and prostitution take place, giving rise to the myth of the immoral, irresponsible black man.

"How can our natives stand to live like that? If anyone doubts the black man is different from the white, he only has to see what goes on in those mine compounds. A white man couldn't survive there!"

Jim, a friend, arrived at a suburban Johannesburg home. The hostess had provided an elegant, bountiful table for her guests. The host, a mine executive, was in an expansive mood. The evening was warm, the guests mellow, content. The host raised his glass of superb South African wine.

"A toast to South Africa, our beloved land. Where else in the world could we enjoy life as fully and live so well?"

The people smiled, nodded, clinked their glasses and looked out over the manicured, well-lighted garden.

"I would be interested in the opinions of your mine workers lying on their cold, hard bunks, as to the benefits of being a South African tonight," said Jim.

The easy silence had been broken, the evening tarnished. Jim was not invited back.

My husband and I were visiting Lesotho. A friend, a priest, invited us to spend a day in the Lesotho mountains with him.

"I will show you the necessities of life today."

We started out on horseback early in the morning. There were no roads to where we were going. We passed through fields of mealies (corn) and were lulled by the rustling of the stalks in the warm summer breeze. We shouted greetings to children at play who stood watching us pass, their noses full of mucus and their tummies full of nothing. We crossed glistening, tumbling mountain streams. We felt heady with the grandeur of the land.

We came upon a hut set in the side of the hill. A tall, blanketed Masotho greeted us at the door and invited us to see his home. There was a small room. We saw two blankets in the corner, a mat, a large kettle, one large spoon, a knife, two plates and a suitcase.

"This is all he owns," said our priest friend. "This is all a man needs to survive. He and his family eat off the land. Mealies is their staple."

"I have just returned from a year in the mines," the Masotho offered. "I am still getting used to all this beauty and fresh air, the richness of the silence and the freedom of my own place."

"Do you like working in the mines?" I inquired.

"I hate the mines. I hate going back! A month here is never enough!"

Startled by the intensity of his reply, I asked, "Why do you go?"

"It is better than watching my children starve."

10

I looked up from breakfast as Mrs. Ntonsheni entered the room. "You were at the church last night," I said.

"Yes. How did you know?"

"You always have a special light in your eyes when you've been to church. The services must be marvelous."

"Yes, not like your white church. You always stop just as the people are beginning to warm up. We sing and dance and lose our tiredness. Last night Mrs. Kekana needed help. She needs to work to feed her children. She didn't have twenty-five cents for bus fare, so she could go to town to look for work. We all gave money until we had twenty-five cents. We had to go around the room three times to get it since it's near the end of the month! A young man talked to us and told us that we were selling out our own people by believing in Jesus, because Jesus is the white man's God. The name the white man uses to keep the black man down. I said, 'Young man, if Jesus is the white man's God, why did he heal my arm that had gone limp like a snake? I asked Jesus to please help me, because I needed my arm to work so my children could eat. When I asked Jesus to make my arm well, he did; and I am very black. Why would he help a poor black woman if he is the white man's God?' "

Mrs. Ntonsheni is a woman blessed, for she has found a sure foundation upon which to build her life, a way to walk that is true and life giving. Not all her fellow countrymen are so fortunate. On one of our trips to Zululand, we met a sixteen-year-old school boy, a Zulu by birth. He told us he felt lost, without a sense of direction for his life.

"When my parents were growing up, they lived in the tribal structure. The elders were responsible for the education of the children. These elders were chosen for their wisdom. The elders taught the children their place in the tribe, their responsibilities toward their parents, the correct behavior of boy toward girl. The chief and his council were the law, the authority for parents and children. The parents were not responsible in the Western way for their children. Now the tribal structure is gone, yet my parents do not understand how to guide me. I have grown up with no culture, no understanding of how to be a man. The school is helping me. I hope I can help my people to learn new patterns of responsibility. The white man took away our culture, but gave us nothing in its place. We ourselves must forge new paths in order to fulfill our human destiny, in order not to be destroyed from within ourselves."

The sad truth is that for many black South Africans, the road to self-fulfillment is exceedingly hard. Too many are still victims of a cultureless world.

The following are excerpts from a letter written by a friend who farms in South Africa.

"I will tell you something of our workers. All the bachelors have left—either from drinking too much or from serious V.D. troubles. Of the seven families we have here, one father has been to school for two years and two of his five children have gone to school for eleven years. None of the other fathers or mothers have been to school at all. They cannot read or write or count beyond three. It means when Robert teaches them to drive a tractor and tries to tell them about the 4th and 5th and 6th gears, they're completely out of their depth. Can you imagine parents with no education trying to cope with four, five and six children of their own?! The fathers have no idea that their money is to be shared with their families. They buy clothing, radios, etc., for themselves—even beds—but not for their wives and children. We give milk every day and meat regularly, and we give the families every male calf born. But from the remarks of the mothers, one gathers that the adults, mainly the men, eat and drink all and the children see nothing. Their reasoning is that they did not have anything as children. How does one explain to people whose brains are deficient through lack of education and malnutrition that a lack of protein in childhood results in a deficient brain? The babies drink from their mothers until they are two, which is a godsend, but I've just struggled with a mother who had a breast abscess and who fed her little chap on porridge (hardly cooked) and absolutely no milk. She and her husband drank all the milk we were providing and the result was a very sick child. It's difficult, as mother and father are charming people and their errors are errors of ignorance, not cruelty.

"I've put one of the mothers, who is an alcoholic, on a daily pill which prevents her from drinking. She was drunk every day and really bad on Sundays. She was very ill, as she would spend nights outside without realizing she was there. She was also raped several times. I told her about the pill in one of her sober moments and she begged me to get it for her. I intend to keep her on this pill until she is well and enjoying the difference and then I will send her for psychological treatment. She is by far my favorite mother here—my children adore her too. She has a golden heart, a dull brain and a strong desire to live (now that she is alive again)."

11

"South Africa is made up of many different tribes and cultures. It is important to preserve the unique identity of each tribe. This is why separate homelands are vital. People of different tribes were not meant to live together. This can be illustrated in any household where servants of different tribes dwell together. The constant feuding creates disharmony."

Thus goes the South African myth. One is

tempted to respond that the same feuding can be found in most any household.

In one of the homelands there is a mission hospital that is a decided embarrassment to the South African government. The people who run the place believe and act on the principle that we all belong to the human family; that while we have an inner tendency toward broken relationships, we were created to live in love with all our brothers and sisters. These people believe it is possible to choose to act in love toward one another and to learn together all this means. The journey is not always easy. There is anger, frustration, pain to deal with, yet great growth and joy and life as well.

It is heartening to see a part of the church being a source of real light in the South African situation. This is not always so. One evening Mrs. Ntonsheni went with me to an integrated religious service. The possibilities for being together at such a gathering were few, so we took advantage of this opportunity. After the service, I asked Mrs. Ntonsheni what she thought of it.

"Mrs. Peace, the man who spoke has been in your home. I never suspected by the way he treated me that he could say the good words he said tonight."

One weekend Henrietta, Jim and I went to
the mission hospital. Henrietta, a black girl,
worked with my husband, as did Jim. We all
felt a need for a time apart on this island
of sanity battered on all sides by the darkness
of apartheid.

It was a beautiful weekend. We played
together, ate together, walked and talked
together. Wonder of wonders, Henrietta and I
shared a room. Black and white are not
allowed to sleep under the same roof in South
Africa. It is illegal.

The husband and wife who run the hospital
are both doctors, both beautiful human
beings. Just watching them go through a
normal day is an exhausting and an inspiring
experience.

Dr. Wilson took us on his morning rounds
of the hospital. Of all the wards we saw,
the ward for children suffering from malnutrition made the strongest impact on me. The
skeletal figures, lying listlessly in small
cribs bore slight resemblance to human
children. Many, hovering on the fragile border
between life and death, had lost all interest
in the environment surrounding them. They
did not even turn their heads or move their

eyes as we passed by. Others cried out
in strange, terrible wails; sitting on their
haunches, rocking back and forth—full of fear
for their strange surroundings and full of the
pain of severe malnutrition. Intravenous
devices were everywhere, as many of these
dear little souls were beyond the normal
process of eating.

I picked up one small, sobbing stranger
and rocked and cuddled him until his cries
subsided. When I reluctantly returned
him to his crib, he fell into a light sleep. The
next child I reached out to shrunk from me
and cried more hysterically. Dr. Wilson gave
me a look full of understanding.

"You can't win them all, Judy. Come,
we must move on."

"These children look so sick, Dr. Wilson."

"Unfortunately, some of them won't
survive. These were in the last stages of starva-
tion before they were brought to us. There
is little we can do to help."

"Is there no way to get them here earlier?"

"Regrettably, our hospital has not the time
or resources to practice preventative medicine.
We are more like an emergency station in
the midst of crisis. This small hospital serves
over twelve thousand people scattered over
large distances. As more people are sent back

to the homelands, the number will increase. We can barely keep up with those who come to us. You have seen the waiting lines of those wanting to be admitted. Because it is difficult to get here, few people come before a problem is acute. We do get out in the district for house calls as often as possible, yet we only touch the tip of the iceberg. We cannot do all we wish, but we do all we can."

Dr. Wilson's normal day starts around 5:00 A.M. and ends well past midnight. He is a man who has reached retirement age and his mission board worries about the pace he keeps.

"They ordered me back to England for a complete check-up last year," he says, "convinced I must be on the edge of collapse. To their surprise, the tests confirmed that I am in good shape. My tests compared to a man much younger than I. I told them I also sleep like a baby."

After dinner, Dr. Wilson sometimes lectures to the nurses on relevant diseases. He lectures without notes and manages to keep the attention of young girls already tired from a day's hard work. He finished this particular evening with a good dramatic reading of *The Snow Goose,* for all who were interested.

Our weekend flew by and too soon we

found ourselves heading home. After many hours of driving we realized we were hungry and pulled up to a café. We all felt the shock of re-entry, for Henrietta could not go in with us.

"Let's have a sit-in," I said.

Henrietta smiled. "I'm not the martyr type, Judy. Just go in and get the food. I'm starved."

We bought meat pies, climbed back into the car and drove off under the darkening sky.

12

It started out like any other day. Mrs. Ntonsheni was washing clothes. Rebecca was playing with the girls. I was straightening up the house. Rebecca, Mrs. Ntonsheni's niece, taught school in Lesotho. She was staying with her aunt while being treated for an ulcer at the local black hospital. For the past two months she had been coming often to spend the day, as she found staying home alone boring.

Harsh pounding on the back door

interrupted our activities. Mrs. Ntonsheni entered the room, her eyes apprehensive.

"A man wants to talk to you. He is a white man that watches us. He wants to see my passbook."

The man who greeted me was pleasant, courteous. He was well built, a man used to being taken seriously, a man without humor.

"Just a routine check, madam. Is there anyone else working here, a boy perhaps, working on the house?"

"Interesting you should ask that," I said. "There was a boy fixing the roof yesterday. Today he is gone."

"Did he have a passbook?"

"Yes. We got him through the Bantu Employment Bureau. Everything was in order."

I did not tell him that David was the son of a friend's friend. He had just come to town and was desperate to make some money, just enough to eat. We had told him to go and sit in the employment office. Dick then went and applied for someone to work on the roof. The bureau clerk suggested Dick choose from the many people sitting in the office waiting room.

"I'll take that young man," Dick said, pointing at David. It is not a simple matter to hire a black man in South Africa.

Mrs. Ntonsheni had gone to her room and was back with her passbook. All was in order. I started back to my work, having been dismissed by the Bantu Affairs man. An eruption of sound caused me to turn quickly. Rebecca was shouting and gesticulating at the black policeman who accompanied the white man. The black policeman looked surly and sounded angry. Rebecca rushed toward me.

"He says I have to go with them because I have no passbook. He got angry when I told him I was a person, not a dog." Her defiance melted into distress. "Don't let them take me. What can I do?"

I looked at the white man, standing clothed in a special calm that is peculiar to officials with authority.

"She will have to come with us," he said. "She knows the laws. She must carry her passbook at all times."

"She will not leave this house and you will not enter it," I said. "You are not a proper policeman. You have no authority to arrest this woman."

He slowly drew his wallet out of his hip pocket, thumbed methodically through his papers and handed me a card.

"The bearer of this card is authorized to

*arrest any suspicious Bantu. Anyone
obstructing said arrest is liable to fine and/
or imprisonment."*

"I still demand a uniformed policeman."

"Very well, madam. Call this number."

I was told by a friendly voice that someone
would come right over. I served us all cold
lemonade as we waited. It was a hot day.
The captain of the precinct arrived within five
minutes.

"You are getting yourself into serious
trouble, madam."

"Couldn't you let Rebecca bring her
passbook to your office tomorrow?" I asked.

"Against the rules."

"What would happen to me if you stopped
me in my car and I didn't have my license," I
asked.

"We would ask you to bring it to the
station within a few days."

"Exactly. So why can't Rebecca bring her
passbook to the station within a few days?"

"Because, madam, she is black and you are
white, and the laws are not the same for you."

"That is what I have been waiting to hear.
I reject a law not based on equality. There
is a higher law by which I choose to live.
If Rebecca goes to jail, so do I. You cannot
take her without taking me."

The awkward silence was broken by the fateful arrival of a reporter friend. Upon pulling up to our house and seeing the police car, he concluded I had gotten into some sort of crazy mess. Bob immediately addressed the police officer in Afrikaans. There was spirited conversation, sidelong glances at me and jovial laughter which dissipated the tension.

"Let me handle this," said Bob. "I will go to the police station with Rebecca and sort out the trouble, then buy these good men a beer."

Rebecca nodded her approval and I consented.

Bob was gone longer than we had expected. He returned alone. The troubled look on his face said all had not gone well.

"Rebecca didn't just forget her passbook. She doesn't have a stamp in her pass-book authorizing her trip here. There was nothing I could do to help her once she admitted that. I did get a promise her case will be brought to trial quickly. She will also be charged with working for you illegally."

"She wasn't working for me," I protested. "She helped out around here because she had nothing to do with her time. She asked for things to do."

"I know that, but the police will find that hard to believe. The charge against you has been changed from obstructing arrest to having a Bantu working illegally on your property. This means that instead of a criminal offense, you are now charged with only a misdemeanor. The difference in sentence is considerable. It's the difference between staying or leaving the country. Of course, you can plead innocent to this charge."

"By the way, what did you say to the police captain that amused him so?" I asked.

"I told him to relax. You weren't dangerous—just a dumb American broad who didn't understand the ways of our country."

"Thanks a lot! You're a great friend!"

"Take your choice. You can be considered dumb and stay, or smart and dangerous and leave."

Rebecca's trial was within the week; the police were true to their word. She was found guilty of illegal entry to the area and working without a permit. If her fine had not been paid, she would have spent six months in jail. She found one week sufficient. I asked her why she had pleaded guilty to the charge of working without a permit.

"I was afraid, Mrs. Peace. They told me I would get out more quickly if I pleaded guilty."

My trial was called within the month. This was the first time I had ever been in a court of law. A friend had come along for moral support. An officer directed me to the front of the courtroom when I asked him for help. The judge was conferring with an aid and took no notice of my presence. I stood before the bench fidgeting uneasily. A friendly looking young man was sitting at a table to my right. He smiled up at me.

"What am I supposed to do?" I whispered. "I've never been in court before."

"Relax," he said. "It's not too bad. Have a seat. The judge will be ready in a few minutes."

I sat down and the judge looked up.

"Stand up, young woman. You are in a court of law!"

The friendly young man looked over at me and shrugged.

"This is a great beginning," I thought to myself. I stood up and walked to the witness stand which the judge had pointed out to me.

The Bantu Affairs officer read the charges against me in the same slow, serious manner I had encountered at my back door. I sensed it was a difficult task for him. He was a basically honest man. He knew I had obstructed arrest, yet he was charging me with another crime, one he also considered me guilty of, but which was much less dangerous to the security of his country. I felt sorry for the man as he heaved a great sigh and sat down. He was merely obeying the commands of men in authority over him.

I just had time to stand to attention in the defendant's dock, when my case was called down. A doctor had arrived to testify under oath that, yes, a certain white woman had indeed been raped. He himself had examined her and was sure of it.

I twisted in my chair to look at the young black boy standing behind me in the black section of the courtroom. He stood with hands manacled behind his back, head dropped forward, eyes brimming with tears. He looked on the young side of fifteen.

"Tell this boy," the judge was saying to the interpreter, "that due to the seriousness of the charge against him, he has the right to appeal his case to the supreme court."

The penalty for the rape of a white woman by a black man is usually death in South Africa. I know of no case where a white man has been hanged for raping a black woman.

The room went still as interpreter's and defendant's voices mingled. The interpreter looked up. The boy shrank down.

"He says he doesn't understand what you are talking about, Your Honor."

There were sighs and moans from the visitors' gallery. The small boy was led back to his prison cell. I pulled my mind back to my own situation with difficulty.

"You say the Bantu girl was not working for you, Mrs. Peace. Yet she came to your house on a consistent basis for two months. Did you, at any time, give this girl money?"

"Yes, I gave her five rand on two occasions."

The judge raised his eyebrows. The prosecutor smiled. The prosecutor, to my astonishment, was the same young man who offered me a seat. He was not as friendly now.

"Mrs. Peace, do you really expect this court to believe that you gave this girl ten rand out of the goodness of your heart, rather than for services rendered?"

"No, I do not expect the court to believe I gave Rebecca the money out of the goodness of my heart. *Nor* do I expect this court to believe I would insult a fellow human being by paying them ten rand for two months' work."

The prosecutor had no more to say.

"Case dismissed," said the judge. "Insufficient evidence. And young lady—"

"Yes."

"The next time you appear in this courtroom, wear a hat; not for my sake, but out of respect for the law."

13

"Who is this?" Dick asked. He had just picked up the phone and heard, "Hi."

"It's Jack."

"Jack who? The only Jack I know lives in the United States."

"This is your friend from America speaking."

"Where are you, Jack?"

"In America."

It was hard to believe, as Dick had picked up the phone to Jack's voice. No operator, no "one moment, please," no pause or static, just "Hi."

"What a surprise! To what do I owe the pleasure of this call?"

"Gay and I were just sitting here talking about you guys. We have a vacation in three weeks and can't think of a better place to visit than South Africa and you. You going to be home?"

"Are you serious?" asked Dick.

"Perfectly."

"You don't plan a trip to Africa in three weeks," Dick said.

"We do. Spontaneous trips are the best. Be seeing you."

By the time we met the Montgomerys at the airport, we had planned their two weeks to show them as much of Natal as possible. We went over the itinerary as we sat on the verandah of a Durban hotel, sipping coffee and looking out at the moon-drenched Indian Ocean. We were all pleased that Dick was able to take time off to go with us.

The two weeks the Peaces and Montgomerys spent together are a kaleidoscope of fascinating memories. There were the days spent with the Samsons on their sugar farm. They are warm, hospitable friends. We spent hours along the Zululand coast finding shells, watching the children romp in the sand, watching the birds do their dances of life. We canoed up the Umfolozie River. When Dick and Jack spotted a herd of hippos, Janet Samson and Dick cautiously paddled back up to observe them. Suddenly a hippo sentry, posted downstream from the herd, charged the canoe swiftly and silently with mouth open. Dick and Janet paddled with amazing speed to the opposite shore, only to be met by a grinning crocodile. Their trip back down the river must have set a record.

"No use telling this story back at the office," sighed Jack. "No one would believe me."

We hiked and rock-climbed in the Berg— Natal's lovely mountains. Bushman paintings were known to be in a cave high up the side of a hill. The way looked long and steep. We decided to attempt it. It *was* a long steep way. Dick and Lisa, our four-year-old daughter, were the only ones who made it to the top.

"This is one story I won't tell back at the office," said Jack as he sat wiping his face and gasping for breath. "It wouldn't be so humiliating if Lisa hadn't made it!"

One evening, toward the end of their stay, we took the Montgomerys to the home of some Indian friends for a curry dinner. Our friends lived in a two-bedroom apartment. They were an extended family of fourteen. Whenever we visited, even unexpectedly, the rooms were spotlessly clean. How they managed this remains a mystery to me. Mrs. Naido had provided a delicious meal. She made a mild curry in deference to our guests' American palates. Even so, Jack sat red of face, tears streaming from his eyes, as he devoured the food. "Sure," he answered gamely, as he was offered a second plate.

We had warned him it was considered
impolite in Indian culture to refuse more food.
The hostess would take it as a slight to her
cooking. Eating is considered an act of
friendship as much as a necessity of life.

Jack and Gay were as surprised as we had
been on our first visit when Mrs. Naido and the
other female members of the family did not
sit down at table with us. "It is not our
custom for the women to eat with the men,"
was the simple explanation. When I had
suggested that I should eat in the kitchen with
the women, as I too was a woman, they
were horrified. "You are a guest in our
home. In your culture it is different. You must
eat with the men. Some of our people eat the
Western way, but we do not feel comfortable
with it."

As we were sipping a sweet Indian tea at
the end of the meal, Jack turned to Joseph
and said, "Tell me what you think of
apartheid."

The room became still. Joseph sat thinking,
then began speaking in a quiet voice.

"How can I tell you what it means for me?
It means being called "boy" at the place
I have worked hard for five years by a younger
man who has just started work and is already
earning more than I am, although he is

less qualified. It means having nothing to say when my little girl asks me why a young white man pushes me roughly aside on the street so he can pass. It means living with a fear that gnaws at my strength, a fear that grows from the knowledge of the contempt both black and white hold for us Indians. Jack, I don't know how to talk to you about apartheid. For you apartheid is an ideology. For me it is my moment-by-moment experience of life."

14

The car was parked along the main road in the location. I watched as school children tumbled out of the bus, laughing, chattering, skipping excitedly along the road. They had been released from school and were eager to play. Two hundred yards farther up the road, people were shuffling up to the black hospital. Many walked with hunched shoulders, a visible sign of their inward sighs.

I had been sitting there in the car for twenty minutes. Mrs. Ntonsheni was visiting a relative to break the news of her aunt's

death and I had chosen to wait in the car.
Through the window, I could see the valleys
and hills of the black location. It was an
especially beautiful spot, this location. The
natural loveliness of the place made the signs
of poverty more stark. Shanty huts don't
belong in the garden of Eden. As I watched the
children, the old people, the hills alive
with sunlight, I was overwhelmed with my love
for this marvelous portion of the earth.
How rich the land, how diverse and fascinating
the people! How good life could be here; how
full of fear and despair it is!

My mind whirled with incidents from the
past, incidents that illuminate life in South
Africa.

There was the morning Mrs. Ntonsheni
came in weary, worried.

"It is Mr. Ntonsheni," she said. "He was
drunk again last night. Why does he get drunk?
He never tells me why he gets drunk."

Mr. Ntonsheni had recently retired. He had
worked thirty years for the city, in the garbage
detail. For thirty years, five days a week,
Mr. Ntonsheni ran after a garbage truck *that
never stopped going,* as he emptied the white
man's trash. At the end of a day, he was
dog-tired. At the end of thirty years he was

worn out. Due to his exceptional work record, the city had given him a retirement pension of ten rand per month. It was made clear to him that this was not the usual procedure, but a special recognition for his outstanding service.

"Why does he get drunk, Mrs. Peace? It makes more work for me. We need the money he drinks up to live. Why doesn't he understand it hurts his family?"

"He knows no other way to handle the reality of his life," I said. "I know it places more burden on you. Perhaps it will help if you understand it is a sign of his own deep pain and frustration."

There was the morning Mrs. Ntonsheni's nephew, Jonathan, came to call. He stopped in periodically to see how she was. I invited him to join me on the verandah for tea. We talked about his plans for the future, his frustrations with the unjust limitations placed on his life. I inquired about his mother's health and we discussed the hard life of a black woman who wants to make a home for her family and fights for it. She lives in constant fear that the home she has worked to maintain can be destroyed by a government edict ordering the women and children to a "home-land" they have never seen. At one point in our conversation Jonathan started to shake his head, then began chuckling.

"What is it?" I asked.

"It's hard to explain," he said. "How could you understand how very strange it is for me to sit here drinking tea with you and talking as we are. It is hard to explain."

There was the afternoon I asked Mrs. Ntonsheni if she had seen my hairbrush. She said she hadn't. Later I found her in the kitchen, quiet with anger.

"What's wrong?" I asked.

"I didn't take that hairbrush," she said.

"I never said you did," I replied, surprised and hurt. "I only asked you if you'd seen it. How dare you accuse me of suspecting you of taking it. How could you think such a thing of me?"

"I'm sorry," she said later. "It's an automatic response. If a white woman asks us if we know where something is, she usually thinks we have stolen it and she wants it back. I still feel afraid when you can't find something. Many of my people do steal things. But I think white people expect us to steal or they would pay us enough to live."

There was the evening we had a black friend

to dinner. At 7:30 I told Stephen, our three-year-old, it was time to go to bed. He was in the midst of marvelous games with William and was reluctant to leave the fun. Our girls followed him shortly with no more enthusiasm.
When I re-entered the living room, having tucked all three children in their beds for the third time, William looked up and spoke.

"This evening I have been related to by white children as a man and a friend, not as a black boy. I do not think it possible for you to comprehend what it has meant to me. Your children have given me a rare gift this evening."

There was the afternoon Mrs. Ntonsheni and I were talking. I answered a knock at the door and returned with a friend. Mrs. Ntonsheni had retreated into the role of silent servant in the few minutes I was away. Once my friend left, I turned to Mrs. Ntonsheni.

"Why don't you let people see who you are? You help perpetuate the silent-servant myth by refusing to show you are a real person."

"You are asking too much of me, Mrs. Peace. I have to protect myself. I can only stand so much pain. If I really showed who I am, most whites in this country would call me 'cheeky.' "

I thought back to one man who had said

just that. "That woman is a cheeky servant. I wouldn't have her in my house."

"You have some friends who are different," continued Mrs. Ntonsheni. "When I know I can trust a person, I let them know me. That is as much as I can do."

There was the day I was teaching *Cry, The Beloved Country* by Alan Paton to a class of South African high-school girls.

"I don't like this book, Mrs. Peace."

"Why not, Marie?" I asked.

"Because it makes me feel like Africans are people just like me. If I really believe that, I will have to act differently than I do to them. I will have to rethink my plans for my life too."

When we had finished the book, Sally handed me a poem she had written. It was called "This Land of Ours."

They were here first,
But the land was greedily snatched away
*   from them,*
And nothing put in its place.
Slowly they drift to the bad world
Of crime, prostitution and drink.

Rich South Africa,
Full of diamonds and gold.
Shares rise,

Men are glad.
For them it means more cars, better houses
But the poor African, on whose back the
    labour's borne,
Still lives in his shabby hut
With his feet for transport
And fire for his warmth.

There were the times we went to visit our
friend, Geoffry. Legally only two people
could be in a room with him at once, for Geoffry
was under a banning order. His wife would
have to leave the room in order for him not to
break his ban. Being caught breaking any
of the limitless restrictions on his life resulted
in a prison sentence. Geoffry had spent a week
in prison for forgetting to report to the
police station one Saturday morning for his
weekly "check-in." He had slept on a
cold concrete floor with one thin blanket. He
said he found the week something of a
relief. It had released him from being his own
jailer.

Geoffry was well educated and was using his
forced spare time to work on his doctorate.
His jobs varied. They could not break any of
the restrictions of his banning order. It was not
easy to find a job where he was never in a
room with more than two people at a time.

Geoffry was banned at seventeen for voicing his opposition to apartheid in ways that were a "threat to the security of the country." He does not believe in the use of force. The ban was for five years. At the end of five years, he had expected to be rebanned and had prepared himself to face that probability.

He was freed for six months. What I noticed most during that time was that he laughed easily again. At the end of six months he was rebanned. His crime—he had not "changed his ideas" and was still considered "a threat to the government of South Africa."

We asked Geoffry if he had considered leaving the country on a one-way passport, rather than endure ten years of virtual imprisonment. He *had* considered leaving the country. It was an attractive temptation, for he had much work he wanted to do. Yet he felt at this time his destiny lay in his own land. If his life served for nothing more than to point out what happens to a white South African who loudly opposes apartheid in his country, then so be it.

There was the time a black friend said to me, "Judy, any white man who seriously follows the way of Jesus Christ in our country will eventually end up banned, imprisoned or thrown out of the country. I don't condemn those who don't. It is a *hard* way to live.''

There was the time we had dinner with a minister friend in Johannesburg. He told us the story of twenty-two black people he knew, detained in prison for over a year, with no charges brought against them. During this time they were all tortured; men and women. Men's genitals were slammed in drawers and the men left standing there for long periods of time. Women were made to balance on a brick for hours and were beaten when they fell off. Many other horrors were practiced in the hope of getting these people to confess. What they were supposed to confess they never discovered.

When the twenty-two were released, most of them had become committed to violence. Most of them had been pacifists by persuasion upon entering prison. Only a few remained pacifists.

Mrs. Ntonsheni glanced at me as she got back into the car. "You have been crying," she said.

"Yes. I have been feeling the pain of loving this land."

15

The car bumped along over the potholes, slowing when the puddles turned into pools. The first time I had driven this road, I had stopped at the bridge, two wide logs across the swollen stream, and wondered if we could make it across. Today I maneuvered the car across with little hesitation. The road, an oversized cow trail, got progressively worse until we could go no farther. We got out, surrounded by curious, slightly annoyed cows. Few strangers invaded their quiet, lovely pasture, as it was miles from town in an out-of-the-way place.

We looked across the valley shrouded in mist, the lush beauty of the place lost in a vague grayness. The loud calls of people from hill to hill jarred the harmony. Standing here on the heights, no one would suspect this beautiful place housed hundreds of people. People without work. People living in sub-human conditions. People who had lost hope. This was a far cry from the showplace location in Soweto, Johannesburg, the township shown to foreign visitors touring South Africa to see the "true condition" of South Africa's black population.

"It's not too hard to guess why the authorities want whites to stay out of this area," I said to Mrs. Ntonsheni.

"Many people do not know how some of my people must live. If they knew, they would be angry! Come this way. I have found the path down."

We wound down the side of the mountain for half a mile. I never tired of hearing the shouts of the women rise and fall and echo across the valley—a strenuous yet effective communication system.

Mrs. Zuma was not in her hut when we arrived. She was in the church. Her children assured us she would be home soon. We walked to meet her in the direction the daughter, giggling shyly, pointed out. We saw Mrs. Zuma ascending the path supported by a friend. Her sightless eyes shined. I stood in awe of her, for she was joyful in spite of all she was enduring. We greeted one another through Mrs. Ntonsheni. We did not speak one another's language. As we walked, I asked if she had made a decision on the craft school for the blind.

"You must know, I am grateful for this chance, Mrs. Peace. To go to school and learn to weave would be a true pleasure. It would make me feel useful. I could send money back to my children. I would not sit idly in the dark. My son, my daughter and I, we talked. My children said they did not want me to go away, for when they come home now, they find their mother. If I left for the school, they would come home to emptiness. I hope you understand. I know it would be good for me to go, but it is more important for my children to have a mother. They have nothing else."

The next time we visited Mrs. Zuma was to be the last. It was still winter, when life was most hard for her. The children recruited their friends to help unload the coal from the car. Dragging the small sacks down the hillside was laborious. We were women and children and, lacking the strength to carry heavy loads, we made many trips.

Mrs. Zuma's neighbor smiled and nodded her thanks. "This will get her through the rest of the winter. She can cook and keep warm now. She cannot hunt for wood with the rest of us. The children try, but bring little. We all leave her a bit of ours each day, but it is never enough. Now she will be free from worry and cold. God be with you for this."

Mrs. Ntonsheni, Mrs. Zuma and her neighbor chatted in Zulu. I stood looking out over the valley. The air was crisp, cold. I could see my own breath. The sky was a rich blue. The green leaves of the trees framed against the blue made me giddy with their presence. "Look," they seemed to say, "the infinite deep is merely a backdrop for our creation." Slowly I sensed the presence of pain. Mrs. Zuma had never seen her valley. The door to visual adoration was barred to her. Mrs. Zuma was one of the truly great persons I have met. She was a lady of importance to me. My eyes filled with tears as I remembered this was our last visit. Too soon we would leave South Africa. I was overwhelmed with the sense of Mrs. Zuma's helplessness, her aloneness, her utter acceptance of her life.

"Mrs. Ntonsheni," I asked as we entered the hut, "do you think Mrs. Zuma would mind if we prayed together before we go?"

Mrs. Zuma did not mind. There are times to pray. This was one such time. I began a halting, clumsy prayer. The depths of my feelings choked off the words. Words had separated us the year we knew one another. The affection had grown in spite of this. The room was filled with a holy silence, and then my feelings transcended the language barrier. We all felt united, loved, cared for, known. We understood we were at one with one another.

It was not easy to pull ourselves away. I chose not to look back as we climbed the winding cow path.

Mrs. Ntonsheni spoke. "Mrs. Zuma said to tell you she did not know she could feel that way with a white woman."

I nodded.

Months after our return to the States, I received a special letter from Mrs. Ntonsheni. "Our friend Mrs. Zuma has died. Her troubles are finished. The neighbors watch the children. The children cannot go to school now. They must work to live. The children say they are alone now; they have lost their mother. They ask, 'Why do we live?' "

16

Too soon our years in South Africa were coming to an end. This had been our place for eight years—our first home together after our marriage, the land of our daughter's birth.

We knew it was time to leave, yet we knew we would be leaving much of ourselves behind.

Mrs. Ntonsheni and I avoided the subject, until one day she looked at me. "What can I say to you? You are taking my babies away from me."

"I know," I said. "You are as much a part of their lives as we are. You have given so much of yourself to them and have enriched their lives beyond measure. What can I say to you to ease the pain of their leaving? There is nothing that will make it easy. I don't know how I can leave you myself. We have known one another and worked together for eight years. I don't let myself think of our going."

"Mrs. Peace, we must both think of your going. The time is coming. I will have to work for someone when you leave. My children must eat and go to school. We must think about where I will work. It is better for me to find a new job before you go."

"I have thought of that. I think I can find you a job with one of our friends before we go."

Mrs. Ntonsheni shook her head. "You will not find me a job with your friends."

"Why not? They all know how responsible you are."

"They also see how I am in your house.

They will not want me to behave the same in their houses."

"Mrs. Ntonsheni, you are too cynical. Our friends cannot help but see what a good worker you are. They may have changed their perspectives by observing us together."

"I am not cynical, just realistic. You can try to find me a job with one of your friends, but you will fail. Many of them are nice people, but most of them are white South Africans first."

I spent the next few weeks informing friends that Mrs. Ntonsheni needed a job starting the first of July. Some said they would have her if they needed help, which they didn't. A few said they needed help, but wouldn't have her. They preferred having someone they felt comfortable training in the ways of their household. They felt Mrs. Ntonsheni had "too strong a personality" to fit into a different lifestyle. I tried, but I was unable to find Mrs. Ntonsheni a job. I finally accepted defeat and placed an ad in the local paper. "Responsible black woman wants housework. Excellent references available." With excellent references, it is not hard to find work. Mrs. Ntonsheni soon had the security of a monthly paycheck once we were gone.

The day we were to leave arrived. How does one leave a place that has been home and people who have been friends. The time had come for Mrs. Ntonsheni and me to say goodbye.

I looked at Mrs. Ntonsheni.

"Life is made up of meeting and parting, of saying hello and goodbye," she said, and looked away.

"How can I leave you?" I thought to myself. We had been together for eight years. We had felt anger and affection, cautiousness and trust, distance and warmth, frustration and enjoyment, depression and hope. We had felt alien to one another and we had felt known by one another. Our lives had become interdependent in so many ways, even while we had feared this. In eight years, we had come to love one another. I embraced Mrs. Ntonsheni. "I cannot say goodbye to you. It is too hard for me."

"It is too hard for me," she said. "I have dreaded the coming of this day."

We both wept.

She left me standing alone in the garden. Walking slowly, with head erect, she passed through the gate. She did not look back.

Months passed. We were settled into our

new home. The children were making friends.
Dick and I were beginning to feel a part
of our new community. Mrs. Ntonsheni and I
were corresponding. I knew she had had three
jobs since our leaving. One day a letter
arrived informing me she had found a new
position.

"This woman is from England, Mrs. Peace.
She seems very nice. I think I will like
working for her. I hope so."

I hoped so too. She had felt restless and
dissatisfied since our departure. It had made me
feel guilty. Perhaps Mrs. van der Merwe
was right. My mind wandered back to the day
we attended a *braaivleis* at her home. It
was a spring day in Johannesburg. The sun
was brilliant, the sky cloudless. The garden
was lush with varieties of plants and flowers.
The van der Merwes were warm people,
people committed to breaking down the
barriers between the English and the Afrikaners.
They were one of the first Afrikaans families I
met living in a predominantly English
community. Apartheid is a cultural, as well
as racial, attitude toward life. I respected
the van der Merwes for choosing to reach
beyond their cultural heritage. This was not
done lightly by an Afrikaner. Their cultural
roots were deep, emotional and brought inner

stability to the business of living.

Mrs. van der Merwe and I were in the midst of devouring sausages straight off the grill. We were discussing the problem of hiring good help.

"I'm lucky to have a woman working with me who has become a real friend," I said.

Mrs. van der Merwe turned her head to look at me. "How much are you paying your servant?"

I was surprised by the question, but I answered.

"That is far too much," she said. "You are making it impossible for her to be satisfied with a normal work situation. You are spoiling her for her place in our society. Every person must accept their lot in life realistically and be content with life as it is. Mrs. Ntonsheni is being ruined for life as a black woman in South Africa. You are doing her no favor."

"Is it wrong to try to act justly in the midst of injustice?" I asked.

"You don't understand. It is a matter of facing reality, not a matter of justice."

"I cannot feel it is hurting her to see her family fed and to send her children to school," I said. "What she has now cannot be taken away from her even if life is harder in the years ahead."

Yet today I feel guilt, for Mrs. Ntonsheni is now dissatisfied. She was not content with the injustice of her life before we met. Have we made it more unbearable for her? I do not know. I only know I would act the same again.

17

It looked innocent enough. Just a thin, blue air-mail letter pushed through the mail slot in our front door. Since living in Africa, we had received many such letters. I switched off the vacuum cleaner, bent to pick up the fragile paper and settled down in a chair to catch up on the life and thoughts of a friend. From the handwriting, I saw this was a letter from Mrs. Ntonsheni. I carefully pried open the glued paper and read with anticipation.

Anticipation gave way to shock. When I finished the letter, I sat quietly, stunned. Slowly the quiet was invaded by the emotion that welled up from deep within me and burst forth into sobs.

This is what I had read:

Dear Mr. & Mrs. Peace & family,

I hope you have heard the sad news about my loving daughter, Rebecca. She passed away on the 25th of September. She was knocked down by a car on the location's main road. She died on arrival at the hospital.
We did love Rebecca very much. She was really a sweet child of the family. But God loved her also to come by His side. I do wish you would really pray for us. I think if you were still here Rebecca shouldn't have had this accident because she would have come with me to work.

I'm not going to work for these people, Mrs. Lewis, anymore because she was cross with me because I stayed at home till the funeral. She wanted me to come to work. I am very sick and very weak since Rebecca's death. I want to stay home till I feel well and get sure that I will never see Rebecca again.

I wish you were all here in these days of sadness. I won't forget this easily because I can't believe Rebecca is dead.

Give my love to all the family.

Love,
Mrs. Ntonsheni & family

Finally my grief was drained of emotion and my mind took over, whirling with thoughts. Rebecca, only seven at the time of her death,

was the youngest of Mrs. Ntonsheni's eight
children. She was especially loved by the
other members of the family, for she was
"the baby" to all of them. Why did it have to
be Rebecca? I thought of the fun she and
Lisa and Jenny had had playing. Rebecca
had been very shy when Mrs. Ntonsheni
had first brought her to our home. But
soon she was running and shouting and playing
with our girls. Prejudice must be taught and
these three children quickly and naturally
became good friends. Rebecca's death would
be hard for Lisa and Jenny to understand.

I thought of Mrs. Lewis. Mrs. Ntonsheni had
been full of hope when she started working
for her: "She is a nice woman, Mrs. Peace.
She is from England. I hope this job works out."

I had hoped it would work out too. Yet I
remembered something Mrs. Ntonsheni had
told me long before.

"My people think it is sometimes easier to
work for white South Africans than for people
from England and America. People from
overseas say they think apartheid is wrong.
They act very nice to us at first. Soon they get
used to the ways of our country. It does
not seem too bad to them anymore. They like
having servants cheaply. Before long they
expect more of us than our whites do.

When we work for white South Africans, we know what is expected of us. They grow up being taught the way they should treat their servants. We don't like the way we are treated, but we know what to expect and how to survive with them. Americans and Englishmen can talk nice, but they can get very hard toward us, living in our land."

I couldn't help feeling that many white South Africans would have accepted and understood Mrs. Ntonsheni's need to grieve her daughter's death at home among her family. Mrs. Lewis, a nice Englishwoman, had come to see Mrs. Ntonsheni as the object that freed herself from manual labor. She had become angry when her easy lifestyle was interrupted by Mrs. Ntonsheni's own human needs.

A few weeks later I received another letter from Mrs. Ntonsheni. She explained that Rebecca had been killed by a hit-and-run driver. The family had gone to the police station to find out who had killed their daughter. When a policeman was asked if he could find the information for them, he had looked at them impatiently. "Don't you know we have more important things to do with our time than to keep records of everyone who is killed? We know nothing of your daughter's death!''

"Mrs. Peace," wrote Mrs. Ntonsheni, "the way that policeman treated us, we could have been speaking about the death of a dog. Why is our country this way?"

18

There was a day, in the city of Johannesburg, when Samuel and I sat down to talk. We had talked before. It had become a part of our daily ritual, sitting at the kitchen table for a cup of tea and talk.

Samuel kept the garden for the house we were renting. He was there when we arrived. We had come to know one another over the past year. You can learn a surprising amount over a morning cup of tea. One of the things I had learned was that Samuel was a frustrated composer.

"Mrs. Peace," he asked one day, "do you know how to write down notes for music?"

"Not very well," I answered. "Why do you ask?"

"I have music going on in my head all the

time. It begs to be let out. I do not know how
to let it out. Sometimes while I am riding
my bicycle it gets so strong I think I will burst.
When I am working in the garden, I feel
quiet. That is why I love the garden. The rest of
the time the music bothers me, wanting me
to let it live for others, impatient with me for
keeping it locked up inside my head. I
have tried to find a place to learn to let the music
out. I can find no such place for a black man
like me. Do you know of a place?"

I knew of no such place. I also knew if one
could find such a place, it would be expensive,
far beyond Samuel's means.

"Samuel, it is terrible to consider the
artistic talent among your people that has been
lost to the world because of the false limitations
placed on your lives."

"Yes," Samuel replied, "it is a truly terrible
thing."

This particular morning we were sipping our
tea and discussing Joe. Joe had entered
South Africa illegally in order to find work. He
was from Malawi. He had come to us for help.
While we could not offer him work, we did
give him a place to sleep at night. Joe had not
found work. He spent his time drinking and
fighting. We finally persuaded him that he

was foolish to stay in South Africa.

"Joe," I had said, "you cannot find work in
South Africa without a permit. You cannot
get a permit without legal entry into the
country."

"If I had entered the country legally, I
would have to work in the mines," said Joe.
"That I could not do."

"Why do you stay here?" I asked. "You
will never find work."

"There is no work for me at home. I cannot
sit and watch my family starve."

"You are not sending your family money.
Now they have no food and no father.
You drink and fight in Johannesburg. One day
you may die on the street. Will that help your
family?"

Joe had been convinced he would be of
more use to himself and his family at home
and we had put him on the train with a great
sense of relief.

"It is a good thing that Joe went home,"
Samuel was saying. "It is dangerous to live
in Johannesburg. Many men die here. Boys
come from the country to make their fortune in
the city. There are not enough jobs for all
who come to Johannesburg. If you are black,
you must have a permit to live in Johannesburg. Yet my people come without permits, for

permits are hard to get unless you go to the mines. It is very hard to work in the mines. It is a living death to my people.

"Some men will not go to the mines. They will not sit in the homeland without work and watch their families starve either. They come to Johannesburg illegally. They find no work. They turn to drinking, stealing, killing. Black men from other countries are not liked, for our own men cannot find work. Joe will live longer at home. It is a good thing that he went back. It is a terrible place, this city of Johannesburg. It is a beautiful place, this city of gold. Johannesburg is a place of wealth and promise, a place of poverty and despair. It is a terrible place, this country of South Africa. It is a beautiful place, this country of mine."

Samuel and I sat and were silent, both lost in our own thoughts. Suddenly Samuel looked up. His gaze was intense.

"Mrs. Peace, you must wonder how my people endure all the suffering, all the oppression heaped upon them in this their country, their home."

"Yes, I have often wondered at it."

"We are a people of patience and hope. While we have hope, we can endure with patience almost anything. We still have hope.

Our hope is this: that God cannot ignore our cries of suffering that come before him daily. He will free us from our imprisonment in our own land. We see America as the country that believes in men's freedom. We hope that America will be used to free us. America will not allow us to suffer so, but will fight for our freedom."

"Samuel, it is a hard thing I have to tell you. You must not place too much hope in America. America has much money invested in your country. It is in her interest to see your government remain stable and in control. I do not believe America will fight for your freedom. I may be wrong, but you must not place your hope there.

"Surely God hears your cries. He is a God of justice, of truth, of righteousness and of patience. The oppressor cannot win in the end, yet the end can still be far off. History moves toward truth and justice, yet history moves exceedingly slowly."

Samuel sat with slumped shoulders and downcast eyes. When he looked up, I could see he was old and tired.

"Mrs. Peace, I said that as long as my people have hope they can endure anything. Yet the day they lose all hope, they would rather fight and die than go on living. My people are beginning to lose hope, Mrs. Peace. Their patience is being drained away. Their endurance is faltering. The end of this chapter of our story may not be far off. I pray with all good men that reason, not violence, will be the vehicle for our justice. May God have mercy on us all.''

There was a day, in the city of Johannesburg, six years ago, when Samuel and I sat down to talk. It is my hope that the patience endures and the talking continues; that reason will win over fear, and violence will be cheated by the positive action of love.

Postscript

God sets before us life and death and says, "Choose life."

In June of 1977, the children of Soweto, the African township outside Johannesburg, stopped and looked at their lives. They said in their hearts, No more, we have had enough. One day, the children of Soweto walked out into the streets in protest at the wrongs heaped upon them in the place of their birth. The children walked out into the streets and died.

They were protesting the mandatory use of Afrikaans in the schools. They wanted

English. English is a universal language, they said. Afrikaans is not relevant in today's world. It is a language of isolation, they said.

The children knew it was illegal to demonstrate. They knew policemen with dogs and clubs, gas and guns would be present. Yet they marched in protest.

Some were killed. People said how awful that the children were killed. What is this country coming to? Afrikaans was dropped as a mandatory language in South African schools.

It has been said that a little child shall lead them. The children of Soweto crossed an invisible, yet profound line that day in June. They looked at their options and chose death. Is the shedding of blood necessary, after all, for the freedom of a people?

In 1977 Steve Biko, young, intelligent spokesman for black South Africa, died in prison in South Africa. On October 27, an inquest into his death was held. During that inquest it was revealed that the night before his death, Mr. Biko had been moved, naked and in chains, from Port Elizabeth to Pretoria, a distance of 750 miles. The autopsy showed Biko died of severe brain damage, impaired blood circulation and acute kidney failure. He also had two broken ribs. Yet the white

South African judge cleared the state of any
guilt in the death of Mr. Biko.

After the verdict of not guilty had been
handed down, an old African man stood
outside the courthouse. The old man stood with
his head down, turning his hat around in
his hands, around and around in his hands.
"This is a terrible thing the white man has done
today. A terrible, terrible thing. We do not
want violence, we want peace. So why does the
white man do this to us? Doesn't he *know* that
we want peace?"

What a people want may not be what a
people choose. Years ago a black South African
said to me, "I live with fear in the land of
my birth. I am treated as a child in my own
country. To let go of the fear, to become free
within myself, could cost me my life. But
my executioner would know he was killing a
man."